How to Ace an Interview Essentials in 10 Mins or Less

Crushing Common Questions, Body
Language Mastery, Confident Answers,
& Pre-Interview Calming Techniques

The Fix-It Guy

Table of Contents

Introduction

Hey Future Superstars,

Are you tired of sweating bullets before interviews? Do nerves turn you into a walking thesaurus, substituting eloquent words with awkward stammers? Fear not! Welcome to the game-changing world of "How to Ace an Interview Essentials in 10 Mins or Less", your express ticket to interview triumph.

Picture this: You, confidently striding into an interview room, armed with a secret weapon, the power of strategic preparation that takes just 10 minutes. No more late-night cramming, no more panic-induced word salads. It's time to conquer the job market like a pro, with a grin that says, "Yeah, I got this!"

In this tactical guide, we're not about dragging you through a tedious marathon of preparation. Who's got time for that? We're all about efficiency, giving you the juiciest, most effective strategies to prep for questions, unleash killer body language, deliver answers that sparkle and bid adieu to interview anxiety like a boss.

So, grab a seat, and let's embark on a journey that transforms interviews from heart-pounding ordeals into opportunities to shine. We've got hacks, we've got laughs, and most importantly, we've got your back.

Why settle for "good enough" when you can be extraordinary? Your dream job awaits, let's snag it together, effortlessly and with a sprinkle of swagger!

Ready to rock the interview room? Let's dive in!

Chapter 1

The 10-Minute Interview Prep

Time-Efficient Strategies

Alright, buckle up, my future interview rockstars! We're diving into the secret sauce of quick, effective interview prep, and trust me, it's as easy as making your morning cup of coffee. We've got ten minutes, a dash of attitude, and a whole lot of confidence to brew.

Step 1: Choose Your Battlefield (1 Minute)
Start by picking your spot. It's like choosing the perfect Netflix-watching corner, but instead, you're setting the stage for your job-winning performance. Find a quiet place where you won't be interrupted by your cat's sudden urge to claim your keyboard as their throne.

Troubleshooting Tip: The Wi-Fi acting up? Find a cozy spot with a good old paperback on hand, we're going retro!

Step 2: Gather Your Ammo (2 Minutes)

Grab your resume, job description, and a notepad. This is your interview arsenal. The resume is your script, the job description is your screenplay, and the notepad is for those genius thoughts that pop up mid-prep.

Troubleshooting Tip: Can't find your resume? Panic not, my friend. LinkedIn is your backup, and it's just a click away.

Step 3: Quick Brain Dump (3 Minutes)

Take a deep breath; we're not venturing into deep meditation territory. Jot down key achievements, skills, and a couple of superhero moments from your last job. This is your cheat sheet, a swift reminder of how awesome you are.

Troubleshooting Tip: Brain freeze? Imagine you're bragging to your bestie about landing this job, the words will flow!

Step 4: Speed Date the Company (2 Minutes)

Google is your wingman here. Quickly scan the latest news about the company, recent achievements, challenges, maybe even the CEO's pet parrot's name. It's all fair game in the quest for the perfect match.

Troubleshooting Tip: Got sidetracked by the CEO's parrot? Happens to the best of us. Set a timer for this step, efficiency, my friend!

Step 5: Power Pose (2 Minutes)

Stand tall, throw your hands up like you just won a marathon, and smile. This isn't just a pre-interview pep talk; it's science. Power posing boosts confidence and tells your brain you're ready to conquer.

Troubleshooting Tip: Neighbors giving you weird looks? Invite them to join, make it a neighborhood power pose party!

Key Takeaways:
- **Location Matters:** Choose a quiet spot.
- **Resume, Job Description, Notepad:** Your holy trinity.
- **Brain Dump:** Brag like you're the hero of your own story.
- **Google the Company:** Be the Sherlock of the job market.
- **Power Pose:** Channel your inner superhero.

Next Steps:

1. Create Your Interview Arsenal: Organize your resume, job description, and notepad.

2. Brain Dump Session: Jot down your victories and skills.

3. Google Detective: Know the company like your favorite TV show.

4. Strike a Power Pose: Confidence, my friend, confidence.

Now go, my interview Jedi! The world is your stage, and those questions are your cues. Break a leg, metaphorically, of course!

Setting the Stage for Success

Alright, my future interview maestros, let's talk about turning your interview stage into a spotlight that's solely yours. We're not just entering a room; we're making an entrance that says, "Get ready, because I'm about to rock your professional world."

Step 1: Arrive Early (2 Minutes Early is On Time, Right?)

I know, I know, punctuality sounds like your grandma's advice. But trust me, it's gold. Arriving a couple of minutes early not only shows you're responsible but also gives you a chance to soak in the ambiance and, more importantly, find the coffee machine.

Troubleshooting Tip: Traffic jams? Google Maps is your co-pilot, reroute, recalibrate, and arrive on time.

Step 2: Greet Your Audience (Cue the Virtual Handshake)

Virtual or in-person, greetings set the tone. A firm (but not bone-crushing) handshake or a confident online wave, make that first impression count. Smile like you've just been reunited with your long-lost puppy.

Troubleshooting Tip: Sweaty palms? Pretend you're an undercover spy, and the handshake is part of your secret mission. Works like a charm.

Step 3: Mind the Body Language (No, Slouching Won't Cut It)

You've heard it before, but it's worth repeating: stand tall, sit up straight, and for the love of interview gods, please don't cross your arms like you're guarding a top-secret recipe. Open body language screams confidence.

Troubleshooting Tip: Got the nervous jitters? Imagine you're a superhero about to save the day. Shoulders back, chest out, you're unstoppable!

Step 4: Connect with the Interviewer (Small Talk, Big Impact)

Before diving into the deep sea of interview questions, dip your toes in with a bit of small talk. It could be about the weather, a recent company event, or the office plant that seems to be thriving against all odds. Establishing a connection humanizes the experience.

Troubleshooting Tip: Blank on small talk? Compliment the office decor, it's like an instant icebreaker.

Step 5: Tech Check (For Virtual Rockstars)
If your stage is a virtual one, make sure your tech game is strong. Check your camera, microphone, and that your Wi-Fi isn't plotting against you. A smooth virtual entrance is as crucial as a red carpet walk.

Troubleshooting Tip: Pixelated face? Close those unnecessary tabs, tell your roommate to stop hogging the bandwidth, and voilà, crystal-clear video.

Key Takeaways:
- **Early Arrival:** Fashionably early is the new black.
- **Greeting Magic:** Handshake or virtual wave, make it memorable.
- **Body Language Mastery:** Stand tall, open up, and be the superhero you are.
- **Connect Through Small Talk:** Break the ice, not your confidence.
- **Tech Check (Virtual Edition):** Ensure you're pixel-perfect.

Next Steps:

1. **Arrive Early:** Set that watch a tad early.
2. **Master the Greeting:** Firm handshake or confident virtual wave.

3. Own Your Body Language: Superhero stance, activate!

4. Small Talk Pro: Find common ground before diving in.

5. Virtual Tech Check: Pixelate-proof your virtual stage.

Now, my interview virtuosos, you're not just setting the stage; you're owning it. Go out there and nail that first impression, you've got this!

Chapter 2

Mastering Common Questions

Understanding Frequently Asked Questions

Alright, champs, time to tackle the battlefield of frequently asked questions in interviews. Think of it as preparing for the greatest hits concert, except, in this case, the hits are your responses, and the audience is your potential employer. Let's dive into the art of understanding the questions thrown your way.

Step 1: Know Thy Enemy (Read: Understand the Common Questions)
Start by familiarizing yourself with the greatest hits playlist. What are the questions that dance into almost every interview? The classics include "Tell me about yourself," "What are your strengths and weaknesses?" and the evergreen "Where do you see yourself in five years?" Understanding these questions is like knowing the lyrics to your favorite song, you've got to sing along.

Troubleshooting Tip: Feeling overwhelmed? Start with the basics and work your way up. Rome wasn't built in a day, and neither is your perfect interview response.

Step 2: Decoding the Subtext (Because Questions Have Layers)

Sure, they ask, "What's your greatest weakness?" but what they really want to know is if you're self-aware and actively working on self-improvement. It's like a pop quiz for emotional intelligence. Decode the subtext of each question, it's the secret sauce to crafting responses that leave them nodding in approval.

Troubleshooting Tip: Subtext got you scratching your head? Break it down. What's the question really asking, and how does your answer showcase your awesomeness?

Step 3: Crafting Your Personal Playlist (Tailoring Responses)

Every interview is unique, just like every concert. Tailor your responses to match the vibe of the company and the role you're applying for. If they're looking for a team player, your response should be like a melody that harmonizes with collaboration.

Troubleshooting Tip: Feeling like a broken record? Mix it up! Take the core of your response and tweak it to fit different scenarios. You're the DJ of your own interview soundtrack.

Step 4: Rehearse, But Don't Sound Like a Robot (Natural Vibes Only)

Repetition is the mother of skill, but sounding like a rehearsed robot is the cousin of interview disasters. Practice your responses until they flow naturally. Imagine you're chatting with a friend, authenticity is the key to winning hearts.

Troubleshooting Tip: Record yourself answering questions. If you cringe, you're onto something. Smooth out the rough edges until it sounds like a conversation, not a monologue.

Step 5: Embrace the Curveballs (Unexpected Questions)

Life, like interviews, throws curveballs. Be ready for the unexpected. "If you were an animal, what would you be?" might sound bizarre, but it's a chance to showcase creativity and adaptability. Embrace the weirdness – it's where the magic happens.

Troubleshooting Tip: Caught off guard? Take a moment. It's okay to pause, collect your thoughts, and then hit them with a curveball response of your own.

Key Takeaways:

- **Master the Classics:** Know the frequently asked questions.
- **Decode Subtext:** Understand what the questions are really asking.
- **Tailor Your Responses:** Customize for each interview.
- **Practice Natural Delivery:** Rehearse until it feels like a chat.
- **Expect the Unexpected:** Curveballs are opportunities in disguise.

Next Steps:

1. **FAQ Familiarity:** Get cozy with common questions.
2. **Subtext Detective:** What's the real question behind the question?
3. **Tailor-Made Responses:** Customize for each interview.
4. **Natural Vibes Rehearsal:** Practice until it feels like a chat.
5. **Curveball Readiness:** Embrace the unexpected with a smile.

Now, my interview virtuosos, you're not just answering questions, you're composing a symphony of responses.

Go out there and dazzle them with your interview prowess!

Crafting Impressive Responses on the Fly

Hey there, interview superheroes! Now that you've mastered the greatest hits, it's time to talk about freestyling, crafting responses that leave your potential employer thinking, "Did they just drop a mic in the interview room?" Let's turn those spontaneous questions into your time to shine.

Step 1: Embrace the Pause (Silence is Golden, Really)
When hit with a curveball question, don't be afraid to take a moment. Pauses aren't awkward; they're your secret weapon. It shows you're thoughtful, not caught off guard. Think of it as the drumroll before the grand reveal.

Troubleshooting Tip: Scared of the silence? Count to three in your head, it's the magic number to avoid awkwardness.

Step 2: The Art of Structure (Intro, Body, Conclusion Not Just for Essays)
Craft your responses like a mini-story. Start with an engaging intro, delve into the meaty details in the body,

and conclude with a memorable punchline. It's not just about what you say; it's how you say it.

Troubleshooting Tip: Lost in the details? Stick to the basics: Who, What, Why, and How. You'll always find your way back home.

Step 3: Think Like a Marketer (Sell Yourself, but Not Like a Used Car Salesman)

Imagine you're marketing a product, that product is you. Highlight your features, emphasize your benefits, and sprinkle them with a touch of charisma. You're not bragging; you're showcasing your best features.

Troubleshooting Tip: Feeling too salesy? Be genuine. Authenticity is your brand, and everyone loves a brand they can trust.

Step 4: Power of Positivity (Turn Lemons into Lemonade)

Even when faced with a challenging question, focus on the positive. If asked about a setback, discuss what you learned and how you grew from the experience. It's not about the fall; it's about the bounce-back.

Troubleshooting Tip: Stuck in a negativity loop? Flip the script. Every challenge is an opportunity in disguise, talk about the silver linings.

Step 5: Mirror, Not Mimic (Adapt to Their Vibe)

Mirroring is about aligning your response with the company culture. If they're all about innovation, infuse your answers with creativity. If it's a laid-back environment, match that vibe. It's like a dance, lead when needed, follow when necessary.

Troubleshooting Tip: Feeling like a chameleon? Authenticity is key, so find common ground. It's a dance, not a mimicry competition.

Key Takeaways:
- **Pause and Reflect:** Silence is your friend.
- **Storytelling Structure:** Craft responses like a compelling story.
- **Think Like a Marketer:** You're the product, sell yourself with flair.
- **Power of Positivity:** Find the silver lining in every challenge.
- **Mirror, Not Mimic:** Adapt your responses to the company vibe.

Next Steps:

1. **Master the Pause:** Embrace the power of silence.
2. **Storytelling Pro:** Structure responses for impact.

3. Marketing Magic: Sell yourself with authenticity.
4. Positivity Jedi: Turn challenges into opportunities.
5. Vibe Alignment: Mirror the company culture.

Now, go out there and drop those impressive responses like lyrics to your favorite song. The interview room is your stage, own it!

Chapter 3

Body Language Hacks

The Power of Non-Verbal Communication

Hey interview ninjas, let's talk about a language that doesn't require words, the subtle art of non-verbal communication. Your body speaks volumes, and in this chapter, we're turning your every move into a symphony of confidence, professionalism, and, dare I say it, charm.

Step 1: The Handshake (Firm, Not a Vice Grip)
Let's start with the classic handshake. It's not a test of strength; it's a greeting. Aim for a firm but friendly grip. Too limp? You risk coming off as disinterested. Too strong? You might intimidate. Find the sweet spot, and remember, eye contact seals the deal.

Troubleshooting Tip: Sweaty palms? Wipe them discreetly before the handshake. And, breathe, you've got this!

Step 2: Eye Contact (Not a Staring Contest)

Eyes are the windows to the soul, right? Well, in interviews, they're also the ticket to sincerity. Maintain eye contact, but don't go all intense staring contest on them. A warm gaze communicates confidence and attentiveness.

Troubleshooting Tip: Blinking is allowed. In fact, it's encouraged. No need to challenge them to a staring duel.

Step 3: Posture Perfection (Stand Tall, Not Stiff)

Stand tall, but not like a robot. Imagine a string pulling you upward from the crown of your head. Shoulders back, chest out, superhero stance activated. Good posture exudes confidence while slouching screams disinterest.

Troubleshooting Tip: Feeling robotic? Add a subtle sway or a small shift in weight, you're a human, not a mannequin.

Step 4: Gestures Galore (Express, Don't Overwhelm)

Your hands are the supporting actors in this interview drama. Use them to emphasize points, but avoid wild gesticulations that could distract. Keep it natural – as if you're telling a captivating story to a friend.

Troubleshooting Tip: Feeling like a mime? If your gestures feel forced, take a breath and let them flow naturally. It's not a performance; it's a conversation.

Step 5: Mirroring (Not a Magic Trick, but Almost)
Mirroring builds rapport. If your interviewer leans in, you lean in. If they're more relaxed, match their vibe. It's like a non-verbal dance that creates a sense of connection.

Troubleshooting Tip: Overthinking it? Mirroring is subtle. Don't mimic every move like a copycat; just go with the flow.

Key Takeaways:
- **Handshake Harmony:** Firm, friendly, and no vise grip.
- **Eye Contact Magic:** Warm, not intense staring.
- **Posture Power:** Stand tall, superhero-style.
- **Gestures That Speak:** Express, but don't overwhelm.
- **Mirroring Mastery:** Dance to their non-verbal tune.

Next Steps:

1. Handshake Practice: Find that perfect balance.
2. Eye Contact Warm-Up: Practice gazing with confidence.
3. Posture Drill: Stand tall without feeling like a statue.
4. Gestures Rehearsal: Let your hands express naturally.
5. Mirroring Dance: Match their vibe without being a mimic.

Now, go out there and let your body language do the talking. You're not just an interviewee; you're a non-verbal communication maestro!

Projecting Confidence through Body Language

Hey there, champions! Now that we've mastered the basics, it's time to elevate your body language game and project confidence that screams, "I've got this!" In this chapter, we're turning your non-verbal cues into a full-blown confidence orchestra.

Step 1: The Power Stance (A.K.A. The Superhero Pose)
It's time to unleash your inner superhero. Stand with your feet shoulder-width apart, shoulders back, and chin level. This power stance isn't just about looking confident, it's about feeling it. Channel your favorite hero, and let the confidence flow.

Troubleshooting Tip: Feeling awkward? Close your eyes, take a deep breath, and imagine yourself owning the room. Now open those eyes and conquer!

Step 2: Smile Like You Mean It (Not a Poker Face, Please)
Your smile is your secret weapon. It's not just about showing teeth; it's about radiating warmth and approachability. Think about something that genuinely makes you happy before entering the interview room – let that positivity shine through.

Troubleshooting Tip: Nervous smile? Practice in front of the mirror. A genuine smile is your golden ticket to winning hearts.

Step 3: The Confident Walk (It's Not a Catwalk, but Almost)

Whether it's a virtual interview or in-person, your entrance sets the tone. Walk with purpose, head held high, and a subtle sway in your step. Confidence isn't just seen; it's felt.

Troubleshooting Tip: Feeling like a runway model? Own it! Strut your stuff like the confident professional you are.

Step 4: Firm Handshakes (Revisited, because it Matters)

We've talked about handshakes, but let's dive deeper. A firm handshake communicates not just confidence, but also professionalism. It's the first physical impression you make, so make it count.

Troubleshooting Tip: Handshake anxiety? Practice with a friend or family member. It's not just about strength; it's about connection.

Step 5: Maintain Open Posture (No Fortresses Here)

Crossed arms and closed-off postures? Not in our confidence playbook. Keep your body language open – arms at your sides or comfortably on the table, showing that you're receptive and ready for whatever comes your way.

Troubleshooting Tip: Feeling guarded? Imagine you're inviting positivity into your space. Open up, and watch the energy flow.

Key Takeaways:
- **Power Stance Activation:** Stand tall and unleash your inner superhero.
- **Authentic Smiles:** Radiate warmth with a genuine smile.
- **Confident Walk Mastery:** Strut in with purpose and confidence.
- **Handshake Precision:** Firm, professional, and memorable.
- **Open Posture Magic:** Invite positivity with open body language.

Next Steps:

1. Superhero Stance Practice: Stand tall and feel the power.
2. Smile Warm-Up: Find your genuine, confident smile.

3. Purposeful Walking Drill: Strut with confidence, not arrogance.

4. Handshake Refinement: Perfect that firm-yet-friendly shake.

5. Open Posture Rehearsal: Practice openness in your body language.

Now, go out there and own the room with your confident body language. You're not just projecting confidence; you're radiating it!

Chapter 4

Crafting Confident Answers

Building a Strong Foundation for Responses

Hey trailblazers, it's time to transform your answers into a symphony of confidence. This chapter is all about building a rock-solid foundation for your responses, ensuring that each word echoes with assurance and competence. Get ready to turn those interview questions into your spotlight.

Step 1: Know Thyself (Beyond the Resume)

Before you dazzle them with your answers, take a deep dive into self-discovery. What are your strengths, weaknesses, and those unique quirks that make you, well, you? Understanding yourself is the cornerstone of crafting responses that feel authentic and confident.

Troubleshooting Tip: Feeling lost? Reflect on past achievements and challenges. Your journey is the raw material for confidence-building answers.

Step 2: The STAR Technique (Setting the Stage for Success)

Enter the STAR technique, Situation, Task, Action, Result. When tackling behavioral questions, paint a vivid picture. Describe the situation, outline the task, narrate your action heroics, and wrap it up with the glorious result. It's not just an answer; it's a storytelling masterpiece.

Troubleshooting Tip: Lost in the stars? Take it step by step. Break down your experiences into each component, and the story will unfold naturally.

Step 3: Highlight Achievements (You're the Hero of Your Story)

Don't shy away from showcasing your victories. Whether big or small, each achievement is a badge of honor. When talking about your accomplishments, let your confidence shine through. You're not bragging; you're letting them know what you're capable of.

Troubleshooting Tip: Feeling immodest? It's not about boasting; it's about sharing your success narrative. Be proud of your achievements.

Step 4: Anticipate the Curveballs (Q&A No Longer a Game of Dodgeball)

Not every question will be a softball lobbed your way. Anticipate the challenging ones. Prepare responses for potential weaknesses or gaps in your experience. It's not about avoiding the tough questions; it's about confidently navigating them.

Troubleshooting Tip: Fear of the unknown? Practice with a friend or mentor. Get comfortable addressing potential challenges.

Step 5: Be Concise, Not Cryptic (Eloquence in Simplicity)

Confident answers don't require a Shakespearean soliloquy. Be concise and to the point. Rambling can dilute your message. Aim for clarity and simplicity, it's the mark of a confident communicator.

Troubleshooting Tip: Words on a runaway train? Practice brevity. Stick to the key points, and your answers will resonate.

Key Takeaways:
- **Self-Discovery Dive:** Know your strengths, weaknesses, and unique attributes.
- **STAR Technique Mastery:** Paint a vivid picture of the Situation, Task, Action, and Result.

- **Victory Showcase:** Highlight achievements with pride.
- **Curveball Anticipation:** Be ready for the tough questions.
- **Concise Eloquence:** Clear and concise beats a verbal marathon.

Next Steps:

1. **Self-Discovery Session:** Reflect on your journey.
2. **STAR Technique Rehearsal:** Practice telling stories with STAR.
3. **Achievement Showcase:** Compile a list of your victories.
4. **Curveball Q&A:** Prepare responses for potential challenges.
5. **Conciseness Drill:** Practice delivering clear and concise answers.

Now, go out there and let your answers speak volumes. You're not just answering questions; you're crafting confident narratives. The stage is set; it's time for your performance!

Strategies for Conveying Confidence in Your Answers

Hey champions, it's time to level up your interview game and infuse your answers with an unmistakable aura of confidence. In this chapter, we'll unravel strategies that go beyond words, ensuring your responses are not just heard but remembered as the resounding voice of a confident professional.

Step 1: Own Your Narrative (You're the Protagonist)
Every answer is a chance to tell your story. Own it with pride and conviction. Imagine you're the protagonist of a blockbuster movie, and this is your moment to shine. When you speak, let your confidence be the supporting actor that steals the scene.

Troubleshooting Tip: Self-doubt creeping in? Remind yourself of past successes. You've overcome challenges before, and this is just another triumph waiting to happen.

Step 2: Pause for Impact (Silence Speaks Volumes)
Confidence isn't rushed; it's deliberate. Embrace the power of pauses. When you pause before delivering a key point, you command attention. It's not about hesitation; it's about emphasizing the significance of your words.

Troubleshooting Tip: Fear of awkward silence? Think of the pause as a drumbeat, building anticipation for your next powerful statement.

Step 3: Maintain a Steady Pace (No Need for a Verbal Sprint)

A confident communicator doesn't rush. Speak at a steady pace, allowing your words to sink in. It's not a race to the finish line; it's a leisurely stroll through the landscape of your expertise.

Troubleshooting Tip: Nervous chatter taking over? Take a deep breath. Slow down, and let the rhythm of your speech reflect your assured demeanor.

Step 4: Eye Contact Reinforcement (The Window to Confidence)

We've touched on eye contact, but let's dive deeper. Maintain consistent eye contact throughout your response. It's a non-verbal contract that says, "I believe in what I'm saying, and so should you."

Troubleshooting Tip: Blinking excessively? It's natural. Focus on the message, and your eyes will follow suit.

Step 5: Emphasize with Gestures (Not a Mime, but Expressive)

Confident speakers don't keep their hands in their pockets. Use gestures to emphasize key points. It's not about a choreographed dance; it's about adding a visual layer to your verbal masterpiece.

Troubleshooting Tip: Feeling like a puppeteer? Keep gestures natural. They should complement, not distract from, your message.

Key Takeaways:
- **Protagonist Mindset:** You're the star of your narrative, own it.
- **Strategic Pauses:** Silence as a tool for emphasis.
- **Steady Speech Pace:** Confidence in every word.
- **Eye Contact Mastery:** The unwavering gaze of assurance.
- **Expressive Gestures:** Adding visual flair to your verbal prowess.

Next Steps:

1. **Protagonist Practice:** Rehearse your success stories.
2. **Pause Perfection:** Experiment with strategic pauses.
3. **Speech Tempo Rehearsal:** Find your confident speaking pace.
4. **Eye Contact Drill:** Maintain consistent eye contact.

5. Gesture Integration: Practice natural and expressive gestures.

Now, go out there and let your answers not just convey information but radiate confidence. You're not just answering questions; you're delivering a masterclass in assurance. Break a leg – metaphorically, of course!

Chapter 5

Anxiety Reduction Techniques

Recognizing and Managing Interview Anxiety

Hey warriors, let's address the elephant in the interview room, anxiety. In this chapter, we're diving into strategies to recognize and manage those nerves, transforming anxiety into a stepping stone rather than a stumbling block. Get ready to conquer the interview battlefield with confidence and composure.

Step 1: Identify Your Triggers (Know Thy Foes)
Anxiety often has specific triggers. Is it the fear of the unknown? Or perhaps the pressure to impress? Identify your anxiety foes, so you can face them head-on. Awareness is the first step to conquering.

Troubleshooting Tip: Feeling overwhelmed? Break it down. What specific aspects of the interview process make your palms sweaty?

Step 2: Breathe In, Breathe Out (The Ancient Art of Calm)

When anxiety knocks, deep breathing is your secret weapon. Inhale slowly, count to four, then exhale. Repeat. It's not just about oxygenating your brain; it's about hitting the reset button on your nervous system.

Troubleshooting Tip: Forget to breathe? Set reminders in your phone or practice mindful breathing exercises daily to make it second nature.

Step 3: Visualization (Picture Success, Not Failure)

Swap the mental image of a disastrous interview with a vivid picture of success. Close your eyes and visualize yourself acing every question, radiating confidence. The mind believes what it sees, make sure it's a blockbuster, not a horror show.

Troubleshooting Tip: Struggling to visualize? Collect positive affirmations and success stories. Create a mental movie reel of your triumphs.

Step 4: Positive Affirmations (You're a Rockstar, Remember?)

Replace negative self-talk with positive affirmations. Remind yourself of your accomplishments and capabilities. You're not an imposter; you're a qualified, talented individual deserving of this opportunity.

Troubleshooting Tip: Inner critic too loud? Challenge negative thoughts with evidence of your competence. You've earned your place at the interview table.

Step 5: Power Posing (Fake It Till You Make It)
Strike a power pose before the interview. It's not just a physical stance; it's a psychological boost. Shoulders back, chest out, you're not just preparing for an interview; you're gearing up for a triumph.

Troubleshooting Tip: Feeling silly? Embrace it. The superhero pose is your armor against anxiety.

Key Takeaways:
- **Identify Anxiety Triggers:** Know what sets off your nerves.
- **Deep Breathing Mastery:** Inhale calm, exhale tension.
- **Visualization Techniques:** Picture success, not failure.
- **Positive Affirmations:** Remind yourself of your worth.
- **Power Posing Confidence:** Strike a pose, boost your mood.

Next Steps:

1. Trigger Identification: List your anxiety triggers.

2. Deep Breathing Ritual: Practice mindful breathing daily.

3. Visualization Practice: Create a mental movie of success.

4. Affirmation Routine: Build a list of positive affirmations.

5. Power Posing Warm-Up: Embrace your inner superhero regularly.

Now, go forth with the knowledge that anxiety is not your adversary but a challenge you're more than equipped to conquer. The interview room is your arena, and victory awaits. You got this!

Practical Exercises to Calm Your Nerves

Hey champions, when anxiety knocks, it's time to open the door with a toolkit of practical exercises. These exercises are not just strategies; they're your go-to weapons to transform nervous energy into a calm, composed presence. Let's dive in!

Exercise 1: Box Breathing (Inhale, Hold, Exhale, Repeat)
1. Find a Quiet Space: Steal away to a quiet spot where you can focus without distraction.

2. Inhale Slowly (4 Counts): Breathe in deeply for a count of four. Feel your lungs expand.

3. Hold Your Breath (4 Counts): Pause and hold your breath for another count of four.

4. Exhale Slowly (4 Counts): Release your breath slowly for another count of four.

5. Repeat: Continue this rhythmic cycle for a few minutes.

Why it works: Box breathing regulates your breath, calming your nervous system and bringing a sense of balance.

Exercise 2: Grounding Technique (5-4-3-2-1 Method)

1. Name 5 Things You See: Look around and consciously name five things in your environment.

2. Acknowledge 4 Things You Feel: Pay attention to the sensation of four things you can touch or feel.

3. Identify 3 Things You Hear: Tune in to three sounds in your surroundings.

4. Recognize 2 Things You Smell: If possible, identify two distinct scents around you.

5. Name 1 Thing You Taste: Acknowledge the taste in your mouth or, if you have a drink or snack, focus on its flavor.

Why it works: This grounding exercise shifts your focus away from anxiety and anchors you in the present moment.

Exercise 3: Positive Visualization (Script Your Success)

1. Close Your Eyes: Shut out external stimuli and center yourself.

2. Visualize Success: Picture yourself entering the interview room confidently, answering questions with ease, and leaving with a sense of accomplishment.

3. Engage All Senses: Imagine the details, sights, sounds, and even the positive emotions you'll experience.

4. Repeat Affirmations: Pair your visualization with positive affirmations about your abilities and readiness.

Why it works: Visualization primes your mind for success, boosting confidence and diminishing anxiety.

Exercise 4: Progressive Muscle Relaxation (Tension to Release)

1. Tense and Release: Start with your toes, tense the muscles, hold for a few seconds, then release. Move up through each muscle group, ending with your face and neck.

2. Focus on Breath: Coordinate each tension and release with deep, calming breaths.

3. Scan Your Body: Pay attention to any lingering tension, and consciously release it.

Why it works: Progressive muscle relaxation reduces physical tension, signaling to your brain that it's time to unwind.

Exercise 5: Affirmation Journaling (Pen Your Confidence)

1. Write Positive Affirmations: Jot down affirmations that counteract your anxious thoughts. For example, "I am well-prepared," or "I am confident and capable."

2. Read Aloud: Take a moment to read your affirmations aloud, letting the words resonate.

3. Carry Your Affirmations: Bring your list with you. Glance at it whenever anxiety creeps in.

Why it works: Affirmation journaling rewires negative thought patterns, fostering a more positive mindset.

Key Takeaways:
- **Box Breathing:** Regulate your breath with a 4x4 cycle.
- **Grounding Technique:** Engage your senses in the present moment.
- **Positive Visualization:** Script success in your mind.
- **Progressive Muscle Relaxation:** Tense and release to ease physical tension.
- **Affirmation Journaling:** Counteract anxiety with positive affirmations.

Next Steps:

1. Create a Calming Corner: Designate a space for these exercises.
2. Build a Toolkit: Compile these exercises in a calming toolkit.
3. Daily Practice: Incorporate these exercises into your daily routine.
4. Customize Your Toolkit: Add personal touches to enhance effectiveness.
5. Share with a Buddy: Practice with a friend to reinforce the techniques.

Now, go ahead and practice these exercises. Remember, calming your nerves is not just a skill; it's a superpower you carry with you into every interview. You're ready to face any challenge that comes your way!

Chapter 6

Real-life Scenarios and Mock Interviews

Simulating the Interview Experience

Greetings future interview maestros! It's time to take your preparation to the next level by immersing yourself in real-life scenarios and mock interviews. In this chapter, we're stepping into the world of simulations, where you'll not just rehearse but refine your skills, ensuring you're ready to shine when the spotlight is on.

Section 1: The Power of Realism

Why Real-life Scenarios Matter
Realism is the key to effective preparation. By simulating actual interview scenarios, you acclimate yourself to the dynamics, uncertainties, and pressures of the real deal. It's not just practice; it's a dress rehearsal for success.

Crafting Authentic Scenarios

Research the Company: Tailor scenarios to the specific industry, company, or role you're targeting.
Incorporate Common Questions: Address frequently asked questions to sharpen your responses.

Include Curveballs: Prepare for unexpected turns, real interviews are seldom predictable.

Section 2: The Mock Interview Advantage

The Benefits of Mock Interviews

Builds Confidence: Familiarity breeds confidence. The more you practice, the more at ease you become.

Identifies Weaknesses: Mock interviews highlight areas for improvement, allowing you to focus your efforts.

Refines Responses: Continuous refinement is the goal. Each mock interview is a step towards polished responses.

Solo vs. Partnered Practice

Solo Practice: Ideal for self-reflection. Record yourself or practice in front of a mirror to observe body language and verbal delivery.

Partnered Practice: Engage a friend, mentor, or career coach to play the role of the interviewer. Feedback is invaluable for growth.

Section 3: Conducting Effective Mock Interviews

Creating a Realistic Environment

Dress the Part: Wear interview-appropriate attire to recreate the professional atmosphere.

Set the Scene: Choose a quiet, well-lit space with minimal distractions.

Time Management: Stick to interview timeframes to mimic real-world constraints.

Feedback and Reflection

Constructive Feedback: Encourage your mock interviewer to provide specific, constructive feedback.

Self-Reflection: After each session, assess your performance. What worked well? What can be enhanced?

Section 4: Incorporating Variety

Panel Interviews

Multiple Perspectives: Enlist friends or mentors to form a panel. Simulating multiple interviewers offers diverse perspectives.

Navigating Dynamics: Practice handling questions from different panel members.

Behavioral Interviews

STAR Technique Emphasis: Behavioral questions are ideal for showcasing the STAR technique.

Storytelling Mastery: Sharpen your ability to weave compelling narratives.

Key Takeaways:
- **Realism Matters:** Simulate authentic interview scenarios.
- **Mock Interviews Build Confidence:** Solo or partnered practice refines your skills.

- **Create a Realistic Environment:** Dress professionally and manage time effectively.
- **Embrace Variety:** Explore different interview formats for comprehensive readiness.

Next Steps:

1. Craft Your Scenarios: Tailor scenarios to your target industry and role.

2. Solo Practice: Record yourself or practice in front of a mirror.

3. Partnered Practice: Engage a friend or mentor for a more interactive experience.

4. Panel and Behavioral Interviews: Mix it up to broaden your adaptability.

5. Feedback Loop: Seek constructive feedback and reflect on each session.

Now, step into the interview simulation arena. Each mock interview brings you closer to mastery. Embrace the process, learn from each experience, and get ready to ace the real thing!

Learning from Mock Interviews

Greetings aspiring interview champions! Now that you've ventured into the realm of mock interviews, it's time to extract every nugget of wisdom from these simulated experiences. In this chapter, we'll explore the art of learning from mock interviews to enhance your skills and readiness for the real deal.

Section 1: The Post-Mock Interview Debrief

Reflecting on Your Performance

Immediate Reflection: Take a moment after the mock interview to jot down initial thoughts and feelings.

Strengths Acknowledgment: Identify aspects of your performance that showcased confidence and competence.

Objective Self-Assessment

Review Recording (if applicable): If you recorded the session, objectively watch or listen to assess your verbal and non-verbal cues.

Body Language Analysis: Pay attention to your posture, eye contact, and gestures. What signals did your body language convey?

Section 2: Feedback, The Constructive Catalyst

Solicit Constructive Feedback

Seek Diverse Perspectives: If you had a mock interviewer, ask for their insights. Different perspectives enrich your understanding.

Specific Inquiry: Pose targeted questions such as, "How did I handle the behavioral questions?" or "Where can I improve my articulation?"

Acknowledging Areas for Improvement

Identify Patterns: Look for recurring themes in feedback. Are there consistent areas that need attention?

Embrace Critique: Treat constructive criticism as a pathway to growth. Every point of improvement is an opportunity.

Section 3: Turning Feedback into Action

Creating an Action Plan

Prioritize Key Areas: Pinpoint the most critical areas for improvement. What will have the most significant impact?

Set Achievable Goals: Define realistic, achievable goals for your next mock interview or the real thing.

Skill Reinforcement

Focused Practice: Dedicate specific practice sessions to target areas of improvement.

Repeat Scenarios: Revisit scenarios that challenged you. Repetition is the mother of skill.

Section 4: Adapting Strategies for Real-World Application

Integration into Future Practice

Iterative Learning: Each mock interview is a chapter in your learning journey. Apply lessons from one to enhance the next.

Variety Incorporation: Introduce new elements and scenarios to continually broaden your adaptability.

Visualizing Success

Positive Affirmations: Use feedback to create affirmations that counteract specific challenges. "I confidently handle unexpected questions."

Visualization Revisited: Picture yourself implementing feedback with poise and assurance.

Key Takeaways:
- **Reflection is Key:** Immediate self-reflection sets the stage for growth.
- **Feedback is a Gift:** Seek and value constructive feedback from diverse sources.
- **Create an Action Plan:** Turn feedback into actionable steps for improvement.
- **Iterative Learning:** Apply lessons from each mock interview to enhance future performances.

Next Steps:

1. Post-Interview Reflection: Set aside time for immediate self-reflection after each mock interview.
2. Feedback Solicitation: Actively seek diverse perspectives on your performance.

3. Prioritize Areas for Improvement: Identify key focus areas for your action plan.

4. Structured Practice: Implement targeted practice sessions to reinforce skills.

5. Visualize Success: Use visualization techniques to envision applying feedback in real interviews.

Now, armed with insights from your mock interviews, you're not just learning; you're evolving. Each session is a stepping stone toward interview excellence. Embrace the journey, celebrate progress, and get ready to conquer the real-world interview landscape!

Chapter 7

Tailoring Your Approach to Different Industries

Industry-Specific Interview Considerations

Hello adaptable interview maestros! In this chapter, we're diving into the art of tailoring your interview approach to different industries. Just as a chameleon adapts its colors to its surroundings, you'll learn how to seamlessly blend with the unique characteristics of various professional landscapes. Let's embark on this journey of industry-specific interview considerations.

Section 1: Understanding Industry Dynamics

The Importance of Industry Research

Company Culture Variations: Explore the distinctive cultures that prevail in different industries.

Industry-Specific Jargon: Familiarize yourself with key terms and industry-specific language.

Impact on Interview Dynamics

Varied Interview Formats: Different industries may have diverse interview formats, from traditional to tech-centric or case-based.

Expectation of Skills: Understand the specific skills and competencies highly valued in each industry.

Section 2: Common Industries and Their Nuances

Tech and Innovation

Emphasis on Problem-Solving: Expect scenarios that test your analytical and problem-solving skills.

Showcasing Adaptability: Highlight your ability to learn and adapt to new technologies.

Creative and Design Fields

Portfolio Emphasis: Prepare a compelling portfolio showcasing your creative projects.

Collaboration Skills: Emphasize your ability to collaborate within a creative team.

Finance and Consulting

Case Interviews: Be ready for case-based questions that assess your analytical thinking.

Quantitative Skills: Emphasize your comfort with numbers and data analysis.

Healthcare and Pharmaceuticals

Patient-Centric Focus: Showcase your understanding of patient care and healthcare trends.

Ethical Considerations: Be prepared to discuss ethical challenges in the field.

Section 3: Adapting Your Narrative

Crafting Industry-Relevant Stories

Aligning Experiences: Tailor your stories to align with the industry's core values and objectives.

Highlighting Relevant Achievements: Emphasize achievements that directly relate to the industry's needs.

Addressing Industry-Specific Questions

Research Potential Questions: Anticipate industry-specific queries related to trends, challenges, and innovations.

Linking Answers to Industry Context: Relate your responses to how they align with the industry's goals.

Section 4: Navigating Industry-Specific Challenges

Addressing Industry-Specific Concerns

Technology Disruption: In tech, discuss your adaptability to rapid technological changes.

Market Volatility: In finance, demonstrate your ability to navigate and thrive in dynamic markets.

Industry Networking and Insights

Networking Practices: Understand the importance of networking within the specific industry.

Industry Publications and Updates: Stay informed about recent developments through industry publications and news.

Key Takeaways:

- **Industry Research is Key:** Dive deep into the culture, language, and trends of specific industries.
- **Adaptability is Crucial:** Tailor your approach to showcase your ability to adapt to industry nuances.
- **Craft Industry-Relevant Narratives:** Align your stories with the values and objectives of each industry.

Next Steps:

1. **Choose Target Industries:** Identify industries you're interested in.
2. **Deep Dive into Research:** Immerse yourself in the culture, trends, and challenges of each industry.
3. **Craft Tailored Stories:** Align your experiences with the unique aspects of each industry.
4. **Practice Industry-Specific Scenarios:** Role-play interviews focusing on industry-specific questions.
5. **Networking in Targeted Industries:** Connect with professionals in the industries you're targeting.

Adapting Your Preparation to Varied Job Sectors

Hello, adaptable job seekers! In this chapter, we're delving into the art of tailoring your preparation to varied job sectors. Just as a versatile toolkit serves different purposes, your approach to job preparation should flex and adapt to the unique demands of diverse sectors. Let's explore how to refine your strategies and ensure you're well-equipped for any professional journey.

Section 1: Understanding the Job Landscape

Diverse Job Sectors, Unique Demands

Corporate vs. Startups: Recognize the distinct cultures and expectations in corporate environments compared to dynamic startup ecosystems.

Nonprofit vs. For-Profit: Understand the nuanced motivations and values that drive organizations in the nonprofit sector.

Impact on Interview Dynamics
Varied Skill Priorities: Different job sectors prioritize different skills. Identify and emphasize the skills most relevant to your target sector.

Cultural Alignment: Understand and align with the cultural nuances of the sector you're pursuing.

Section 2: Common Job Sectors and Tailored Strategies

Sales and Marketing Roles

Demonstrating Persuasion Skills: In sales, emphasize your ability to influence and persuade.

Highlighting Creativity: In marketing, showcase your creative thinking and strategic approach.

Human Resources and Administration Positions

Emphasizing People Skills: For HR, highlight your interpersonal and conflict resolution skills.

Efficiency and Organization: In administration, showcase your organizational prowess and attention to detail.

Technology and IT Positions

Technical Competence: In tech roles, emphasize your technical skills and adaptability to evolving technologies.

Problem-Solving: Showcase your problem-solving abilities, crucial in the ever-evolving tech landscape.

Healthcare and Social Services Jobs

Empathy and Compassion: In healthcare, highlight your empathy and patient-centered focus.

Advocacy and Community Engagement: For social services, emphasize your commitment to advocacy and community welfare.

Section 3: Adapting Your Resume and Cover Letter

Customizing Your Resume

Highlighting Relevant Skills: Tailor your resume to showcase skills most sought after in your target sector.

Quantifying Achievements: Use metrics and quantifiable results to demonstrate your impact.

Crafting a Sector-Specific Cover Letter

Research is Key: Understand the sector's challenges and goals. Reflect on this knowledge in your cover letter.

Showcasing Alignment: Explicitly state how your skills and values align with the sector's objectives.

Section 4: Sector-Specific Networking and Professional Development

Networking Practices

Industry Events and Forums: Attend events and join forums specific to your target sector.

LinkedIn Engagement: Connect with professionals in your desired sector on LinkedIn and engage in sector-specific discussions.

Continuous Learning in Your Field

Sector-Related Certifications: Pursue certifications relevant to your target sector.

Stay Informed: Regularly read sector-specific publications and blogs to stay abreast of trends.

Key Takeaways:
- *Research Each Sector:* Deep dive into the unique characteristics and expectations of various job sectors.

- **Adapt Your Skill Emphasis:** Tailor your skills showcase to align with the priorities of your target sector.
- **Customize Your Documents:** Modify your resume and cover letter to speak directly to the requirements of each sector.

Next Steps:

1. Identify Target Sectors: Determine the job sectors you're interested in.

2. In-Depth Sector Research: Understand the specific demands and cultures of each sector.

3. Skill Alignment: Adjust your skills emphasis based on the expectations of your target sector.

4. Customize Your Documents: Tailor your resume and cover letter for each sector.

5. Networking in Targeted Sectors: Engage with professionals in your desired sectors through networking.

Now, armed with sector-specific insights, you're not just a job seeker; you're a strategic navigator of diverse professional landscapes. Embrace the versatility, adapt your approach, and set sail toward the career destination of your choice!

Chapter 8

Post-Interview Strategies

Evaluating Your Performance

Greetings interview virtuosos! In this crucial chapter, we're delving into the post-interview phase, where self-reflection becomes your compass for improvement. After the interview curtain falls, the spotlight shifts to evaluating your performance. Let's explore strategies to dissect your experience, learn from it, and refine your approach for the next act.

Section 1: Immediate Post-Interview Reflection

Capture Initial Impressions

Record Your Thoughts: Soon after the interview, jot down your immediate impressions, emotions, and any standout moments.

Gut Feeling Analysis: Trust your instincts. What gut feelings did you have during the interview?

Evaluate Your Confidence and Presence

Body Language Recap: Reflect on your non-verbal cues. Did you maintain eye contact? Was your posture confident?

Vocal Tone Analysis: Consider your tone and pitch. Did you convey enthusiasm and confidence?

Section 2: Analyzing Your Responses

Review Your Answers

Strength Identification: Identify responses where you felt particularly strong. What elements contributed to this?

Weakness Acknowledgment: Recognize areas where you felt less confident. What challenges did you encounter?

Assessing Content Relevance

Alignment with Job Requirements: Evaluate how well your responses aligned with the key requirements of the job.

Highlighting Achievements: Did you effectively highlight relevant achievements and experiences?

Section 3: Feedback Solicitation

Seeking Constructive Feedback

Contact Interviewers: If possible, reach out to the interviewers for feedback. Request insights on both strengths and areas for improvement.

Utilizing Mentorship: Engage mentors or trusted peers for an external perspective on your performance.

Constructive Criticism Reception

Open-Minded Approach: Approach feedback with an open mind, viewing it as a tool for growth.

Identifying Patterns: Look for recurring themes or consistent feedback across multiple interviews.

Section 4: Identifying Lessons and Growth Areas

Key Takeaways
- **Success Analysis:** Identify what worked well and contributed to a positive impression.

- **Improvement Opportunities:** Pinpoint specific areas that require attention and refinement.

Constructing an Action Plan

Prioritize Areas for Development: Focus on the most critical improvement areas first.

Skill Reinforcement: Devise a plan to reinforce and enhance your strengths.

Section 5: Maintaining a Growth Mindset

Embracing Continuous Improvement

Learning from Mistakes: Understand that mistakes are stepping stones to growth.

Adopting a Growth Mindset: Embrace challenges and setbacks as opportunities to learn and evolve.

Future Interview Preparation Adjustment

Refining Your Approach: Adjust your preparation strategy based on the lessons learned from this interview.

Implementing Feedback: Incorporate feedback into your practice sessions for ongoing improvement.

Key Takeaways:
- **Immediate Reflection:** Capture initial thoughts and feelings post-interview.
- **Response Analysis:** Evaluate the effectiveness of your answers and content relevance.
- **Feedback Solicitation:** Seek constructive feedback from interviewers or trusted mentors.
- **Identifying Lessons:** Recognize key takeaways and areas for growth.
- **Growth Mindset Adoption:** Embrace mistakes as opportunities for improvement.

Next Steps:

1. **Immediate Reflection:** Record your initial impressions and emotions.
2. **Response Analysis:** Evaluate the strengths and weaknesses of your answers.
3. **Feedback Solicitation:** Reach out to interviewers or mentors for insights.
4. **Identifying Lessons:** Pinpoint key takeaways and growth areas.

5. Action Plan Construction: Develop a plan to address improvement areas and reinforce strengths.

Follow-Up Best Practices

Hello post-interview champions! In this pivotal chapter, we're delving into the art of follow-up, transforming your interview finale into a strategic encore. As you step off the interview stage, your follow-up performance becomes the lasting melody in the minds of decision-makers. Let's explore the best practices to ensure your follow-up is not just a note but a symphony of professionalism and enthusiasm.

Section 1: Timely Gratitude

Same-Day Thank-You Email

Promptness Matters: Send a thank-you email on the same day as your interview. It's a swift, impactful gesture.

Express Sincere Gratitude: Open with genuine thanks for the opportunity and appreciation for the interviewer's time.

Content Specificity

Individual Acknowledgment: If you met with multiple interviewers, tailor your thank-you notes to each, acknowledging their unique contributions.

Highlight Key Interactions: Reference specific moments or discussions that stood out during the interview.

Section 2: Crafting a Personal Connection

Individualized Messaging

Customize Your Tone: Tailor the tone of your message to match the rapport established during the interview.

Reference Shared Interests: If you discovered common interests, subtly weave them into your thank-you note for a personal touch.

Reiterating Your Value Proposition

Reaffirm Fit: Remind them of your alignment with the company culture and how your skills address the role's requirements.

Highlight Unique Qualities: Reinforce unique qualities or experiences that set you apart as a valuable candidate.

Section 3: Multichannel Strategy
Email Etiquette

Professional Subject Line: Craft a concise subject line, such as "Thank You for the Interview Opportunity," for clarity.

Professional Tone: Maintain a professional tone throughout the email, balancing warmth and formality.

Strategic LinkedIn Connection

Connection Request: If not already connected, send a personalized connection request on LinkedIn.

Post-Connection Follow-Up: After connecting, express gratitude again and reiterate your interest in the role.

Section 4: Strategic Timing for Subsequent Follow-Ups

Initial Thank-You Email

Same-Day Delivery: Ensure your initial thank-you email is promptly delivered, capitalizing on the positive momentum generated during the interview.

Subsequent Follow-Ups

Within a Week: If no decision timeframe is provided, consider a follow-up within a week to express continued interest.

Updates and Materials: Share relevant updates or additional materials if you've achieved noteworthy accomplishments post-interview.

Section 5: Professional Persistence and Closure

Respectful Inquiry Timing

Respecting Agreed Timeframes: Allow the agreed-upon time for a response before sending follow-ups.

Polite Inquiry Language: When following up, use polite language that respects the interviewer's schedule.

Graceful Closure Acknowledgment

Expressing Gratitude for Offers: If you receive an offer, express sincere gratitude for the opportunity.

Thanking for the Experience: If not selected, thank them for the experience and inquire about future considerations.

Key Takeaways:
- **Timeliness is Key:** Send a thank-you email promptly after the interview.

- **Personalization Matters:** Customize messages for each interviewer and reference shared interests.
- **Multichannel Approach:** Utilize both email and LinkedIn strategically for follow-up.
- **Strategic Timing:** Follow up within a week for ongoing interest expression.
- **Polite Persistence:** Be patient and respectful in your follow-up inquiries.

Next Steps:

1. **Same-Day Thank-You Email:** Draft and send a thank-you email on the day of your interview.
2. **Personalized Messages:** Tailor your messages for each interviewer, emphasizing shared interests and values.
3. **Strategic LinkedIn Connection:** Connect on LinkedIn and follow up with a message expressing ongoing interest.
4. **Timely Follow-Ups:** Strategically follow up within a week, respecting response timeframes.
5. **Professional Closure:** Express gratitude, whether for an offer or the opportunity, and inquire about next steps.

Now, armed with follow-up finesse, you're not just a candidate; you're a candidate who leaves a lasting impression. Your post-interview communications are the final brushstrokes on your professional canvas. Craft them with care, express your genuine enthusiasm, and await the applause for a performance well done!

Conclusion

Congratulations, future interview conquerors! As we conclude this journey together, armed with the insights from "How to Ace an Interview Essentials in 10 Mins or Less," remember that you're not just equipped; you're empowered to shape your professional destiny.

In these pages, we've navigated the intricacies of interview preparation with efficiency and finesse. From the 10-minute interview prep strategies to mastering common questions, projecting confidence through body language, and tailoring your approach to different industries, you've absorbed a wealth of practical wisdom. The real-life scenarios, mock interviews, and anxiety reduction techniques have transformed you into a confident and resilient interviewee.

The post-interview phase, explored in-depth in the follow-up best practices chapter, is where you cement your impression. It's not just about expressing gratitude but strategically positioning yourself for success. Remember, it's not just about the job; it's about showcasing your unique value proposition to the world.

As you navigate the professional landscape, embrace the art of continuous improvement. Learning from mock interviews, adapting your preparation to varied job sectors, and evaluating your performance post-interview are not just steps; they're part of an ongoing journey toward mastery.

Now, armed with the follow-up best practices, you're ready for the grand finale. Your thank-you notes, both via email and LinkedIn, are your final strokes on the canvas of your interview story. Craft them with care, ensuring they echo the enthusiasm and professionalism you brought to the interview room.

In closing, remember that acing an interview is not just a skill; it's a mindset. It's about confidently presenting your authentic self, navigating challenges with grace, and leaving a lasting impression. Whether you're stepping into the corporate realm, the tech industry, or any sector of your choice, you now possess the tools to not just survive but thrive in the interview arena.

So, go ahead, embark on your professional journey with newfound confidence. Use the lessons from these pages to propel yourself toward success. Your future is waiting, and with the essentials gleaned from this guide, you're well-prepared to ace any interview in 10 minutes or less.

Here's to your success, your growth, and your ability to ace every interview that comes your way. Go forth and conquer, interview maestros!